Colección García - Ledo

D'Har Services
P.O. Box 290
Yelm, Wa 98597
www.dharservices.com
info@dharservices.com
webmaster@dharservices.com
dharservices@gmail.com
Derechos de autor © 2013 Colección Garcia-Ledo
Carátula© Xiomara García
Art and some Photografies send by Colección Garcia –Ledo

Photografies by Juanc - pgs:10,14,16,34,40,48,50,62,70,78,82,84,85,86

Photografies DT/ ID: 10402070,16240908

ISBN-13: 978-1-939948-03-8

All rights reserved. No part of this book may be reproduced in any form or by any means, including photographic, photocopying, or electronic process or in the form of a phonographic recording; nor may it be stored in a retrieval system, transmitted, or otherwise be copied for public or private use-other than for "fair use" as brief quotations embodied in articles and reviews, without permission in written from the author.

Todos los derechos de autor están reservados. Este libro no se puede reproducir completo o por partes, o traducir a cualquier idioma por medios electrónicos, mecánicos, fotocopiado, o ningún otro sistema sin la previa autorización por escrito del autor, excepto por alguna persona que use pasajes como referencia.

Fruits and Their Vitamins

With love, I dedicate this book to all the children of the world.

Frutas y Sus Vitaminas

Con todo cariño dedico este libro a los niños del mundo.

Maria Luisa Garcia-Ledo

Children, I invite you to have fun coloring and learning about spices and fruits, their different kinds and names in Ingles and Spanish. You will learn the importance of their vitamins, which are essential for good nutrition and growth.

Niños los invito a que se diviertan coloreando, además aprenderán sobre las frutas y las especies y sus nombres en Ingles y español, sabrán la importancia de sus vitaminas las cuales son esenciales para una buena nutrición y crecimiento.

Index – Índice

English «Ingles» & Spanish «Español»

Fruits................ Frutas 7

Anon	Anon	8/9
Apple	Manzana	10/11
Apricot	Durazno	12/13
Avocado	Aguacate	14/15
Banana	Banana	16/17
Blackberry	Mora	18/19
Blueberry	Arandano	20/21
Cashew	Marañon	22/23
Cherry	Cereza	24/25
Chesnut	Castaña	26/27
Chirimoya	Chirimoya	28/29
Coconut	Coco	30/31
Fig	Higo	32/33
Grapes	Uvas	34/35
Guava	Guayaba	36/37
Hazelnut	Avellana	38/39
Kiwi	Kiwi	40/41
Lemon	Limón	42/43
Lime	Lima	44/45
Mamey	Mamey	46/47
Mango	Mango	48/49
Melon	Melón	50/51

Orange	Naranja	52/53
Papaya	Papaya	54/55
Peach	Melocotón	56/57
Penaut	Mani	58/59
Pear	Pera	60/61
Pineapple	Piña	62/63
Plum-prune	Ciruela y Ciruela Pasa	64/65
Raisins	Pasas	66/67
Soursop	Guanabana	68/69
Stranberry	Fresa	70/71
Tangarine	Mandarina	72/73
Walnut	Nuez	74/75

Spices .... Especies 77

Bay leaf	Laurel	78/79
Black Pepper	Pimienta Negra	80/81
Cilantro	Cilantro	82/83
Cinnamon	Canela	84/85
Cloves	Clavos	86/87
Cumin	Comino	87/88
Garlic	Ajo	89/90
Oregano	Orégano	91/92
Parsley	Perejil	93/94
Rosemary	Romero	95/96

ANON

Vitamins: A, B8, B12, C, K

ANON

VITAMINAS: A, B8, B12, C, K

APPLE

Vitamins: A, B1, B2, B3, B6, C

MANZANA

VITAMINAS: A, B1, B2, B3, B6, C

APRICOT

Vitamins: A, B1, B2, B15, C

DURAZNO

VITAMINAS: A, B1, B2, B15, C

AVOCADO

Vitamins: B, B6, C, E

AGUACATE

VITAMINAS: B, B6, C, E

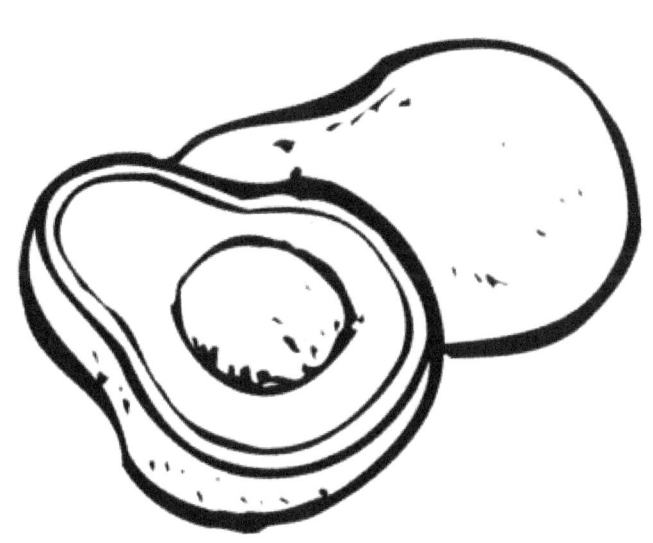

BANANA

Vitamins: A, B, B6, C

BANANA

VITAMINS: A, B, B6, C

BLACKBERRY

Vitamins: A, B, C, E

MORA

VITAMINAS: A, B, C, E

BLUEBERRY

Vitamins: A, C

ARANDANO

VITAMINAS: A, C

CASHEW

Vitamins: B, B1, B2, C, E

MARAÑON

VITAMINAS: B, B1, B2, C, E

CHERRY

Vitamins: A, B1, B2, B3, B6, C, P

CEREZA

VITAMINAS: A, B1, B2, B3, B6, C, P

CHESNUT

Vitamins: B1, B2, B3, B6, E

CASTAÑA

VITAMINAS: B1, B2, B3, B6, E

CHIRIMOYA

Vitamins: A, C

CHIRIMOYA

VITAMINAS: A, C

COCONUT

Vitamins: A, B1, B2, E

COCO

VITAMINAS: A, B1, B2, E

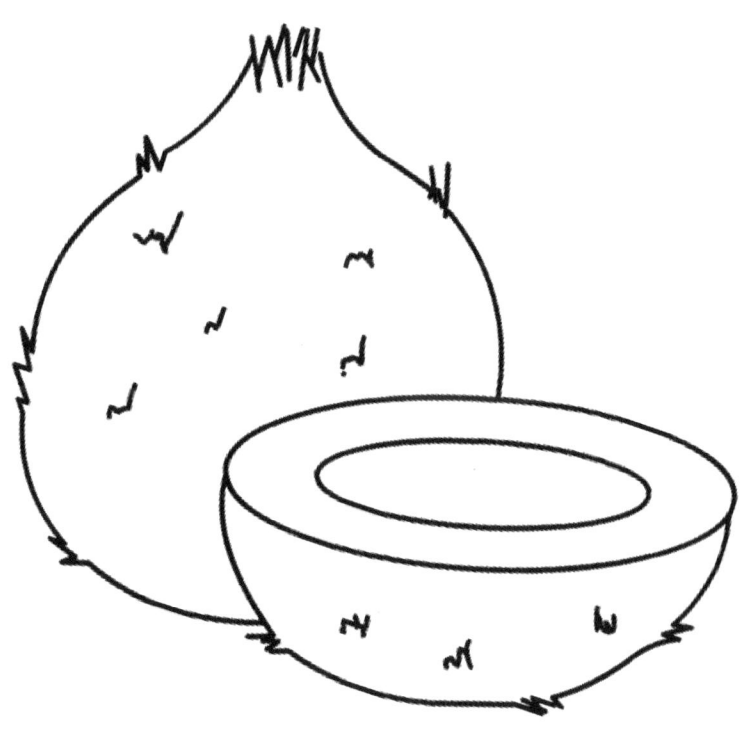

FIG

Vitamins: A, B1, B2, B3, B6, C

HiGO

ViTAMiNAS: A, B1, B2, B3, B6, C

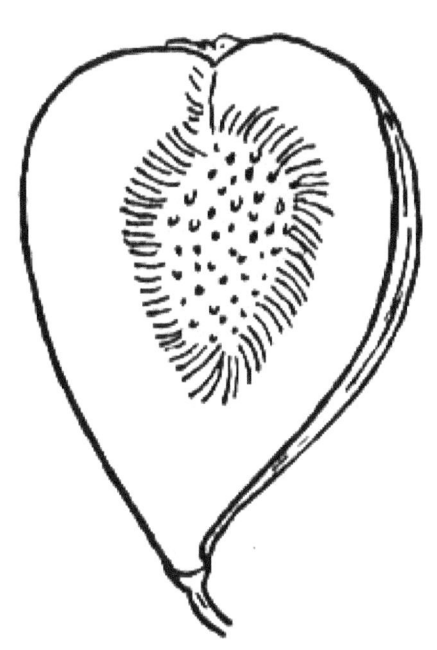

GRAPES

Vitamins: A, B1, B2, B6, C, E

UVA

VITAMINAS: A, B1, B2, B6, C, E

GUAVA

Vitamins: A, B1, B2, B12, E

GUAYABA

VITAMINAS: A, B1, B2, B12, E

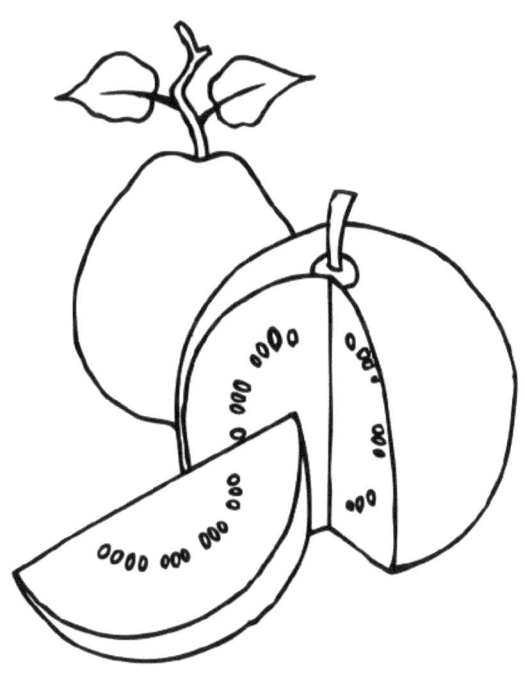

HAZELNUT

Vitamins: A, B1, B6, E

AVELLANA

VITAMINAS: A, B1, B6, E

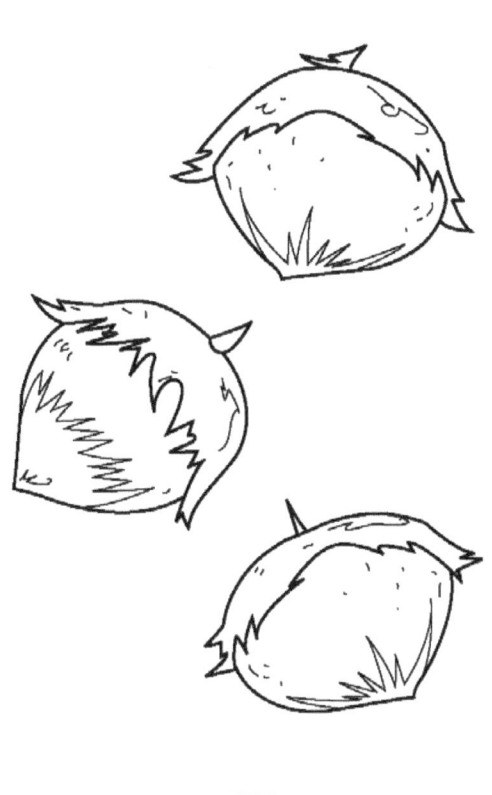

KIWI

Vitamins: C, E

KIWI

VITAMINAS: C, E

LEMON

Vitamins: A, C, E, P

LIMON

VITAMINAS: A, C, E, P

LIME

Vitamins: C

LIMA

VITAMINA: C

MAMEY

Vitamins: A, E, P

MAMEY

VITAMINAS: A, E, P

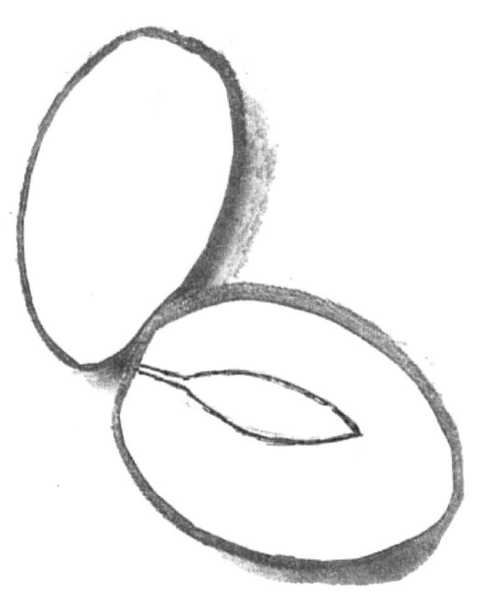

MANGO

Vitamins: A, C

MANGO

VITAMINAS: A, C

MELON

Vitamins: A, B1, B2, B3, B6, C

MELON

VITAMINAS: A, B1, B2, B3, B6, C

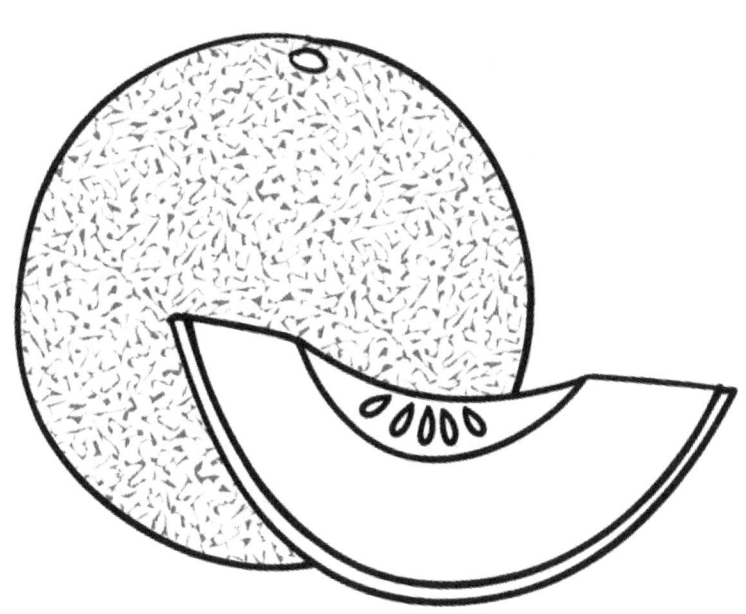

ORANGE

Vitamins: A, C, P

NARANJA

VITAMINAS: A, C, P

PAPAYA

Vitamins: A, B1, B2, B3, C

PAPAYA

VITAMINAS: A, B1, B2, B3, C

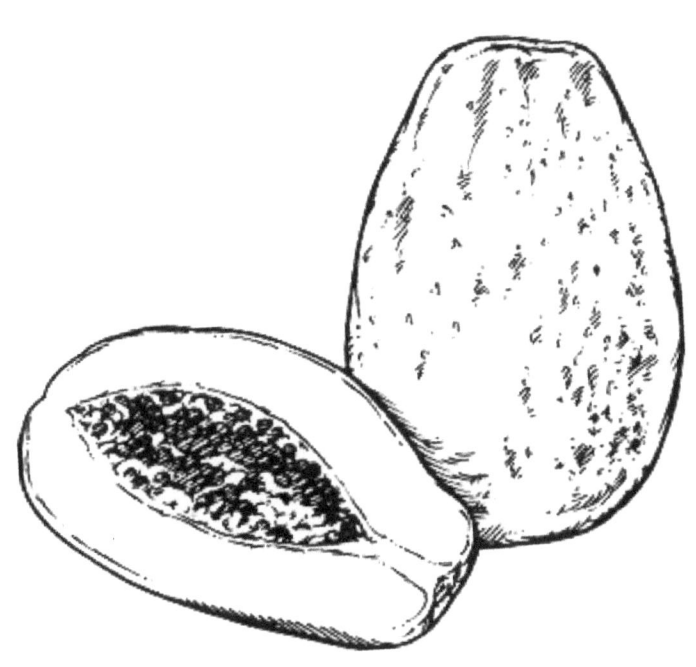

PEACH

Vitamins: A, B1, B2, C, E

MELOCOTON

VITAMINAS: A, B1, B2, C, E

PENAUT

Vitamins: E

MANI

VITAMINAS: E

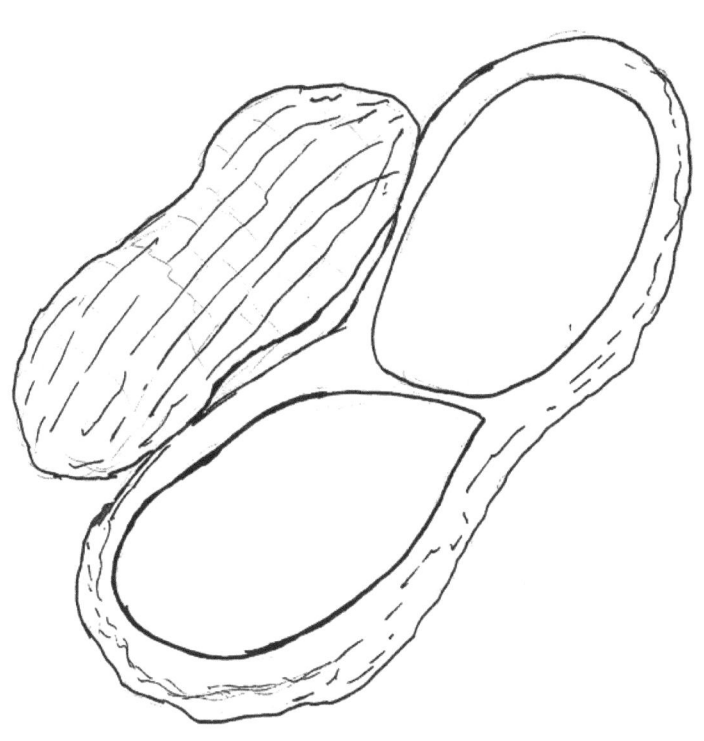

PEAR

Vitamins: A, B, C, D, E

PERA

VITAMINAS: A, B, C, D, E

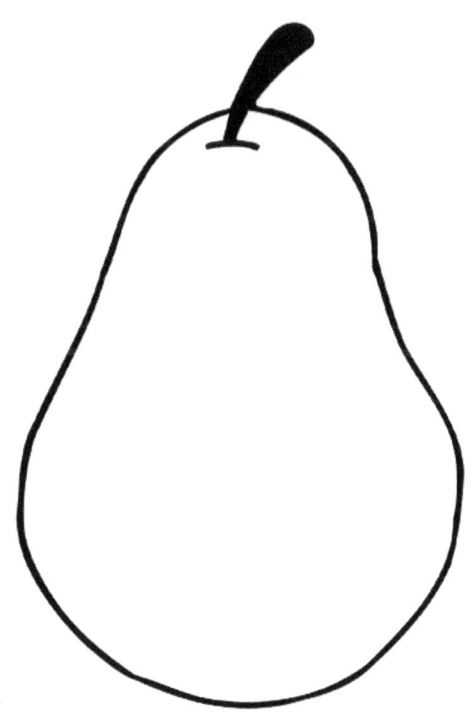

PINEAPPLE

Vitamins: B1, B6, C

PIÑA

VITAMINAS: B1, B6, C

PLUM - PRUNE

Vitamins: B, E, P

CIRUELA & CIRUELA PASA

VITAMINAS: B, E, P

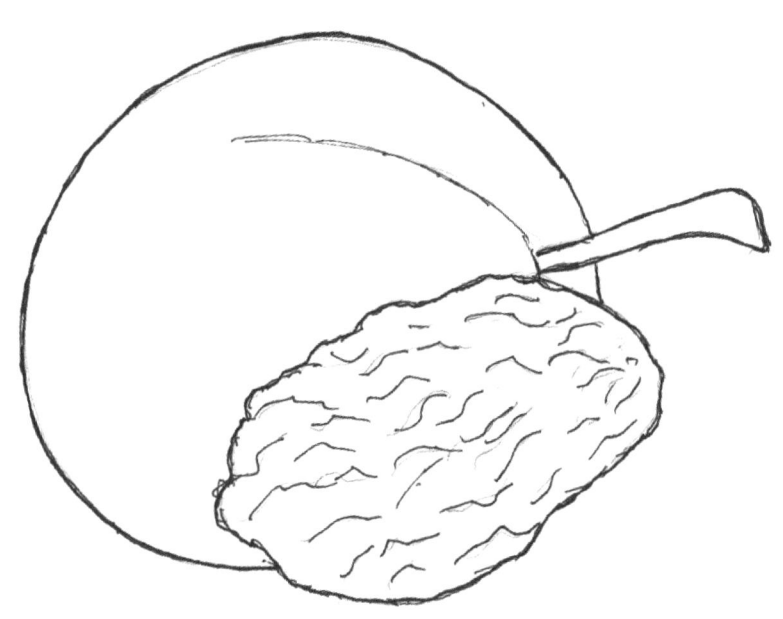

RAISINS

Vitamins: B, C

PASAS

VITAMINAS: B, C

SOURSOP

Vitamins: B1, B2, C

GUANABANA

VITAMINAS: B1, B2, C

STRANBERRY

Vitamins: B1, B2, B3, B6, C, E

FRESA

VITAMINAS: B1, B2, B3, B6, C, E

TANGARINE

Vitamins: A, B1, B2, B3, B6, C, P

MANDARINA

VITAMINAS: A, B1, B2, B3, B6, C, P

WALNUT

Vitamins: A, B1, B6, E

NUEZ

VITAMINAS: A, B1, B6, E

SPICES

ESPECIES

BAY LEAF

Vitamins: A, B6, C

LAUREL

VITAMINAS: A, B6, C

BLACK PEPPER

Vitamins: K

PIMIENTA NEGRA

VITAMIN: K

CILANTRO

Vitamins: A, B1, B2, C

CILANTRO

VITAMINAS: A, B1, B2, C

CINNAMON

Vitamins: A, B1, B3, C

CANELA

VITAMINAS: A, B1, B3, C

CLOVES

Vitamins: A, C, E, K

CLAVOS

VITAMINAS: A, C, E, K

CUMIN

Vitamins: A, C, E

COMINO

VITAMINAS: A, C, E

GARLIC

Vitamins: A, B, B1, B3, B6, C

AJO

VITAMINAS: A, B, B1, B3, B6, C

OREGANO

Vitamins: A, B1, B9

ORÉGANO

VITAMINAS: A, B1, B9

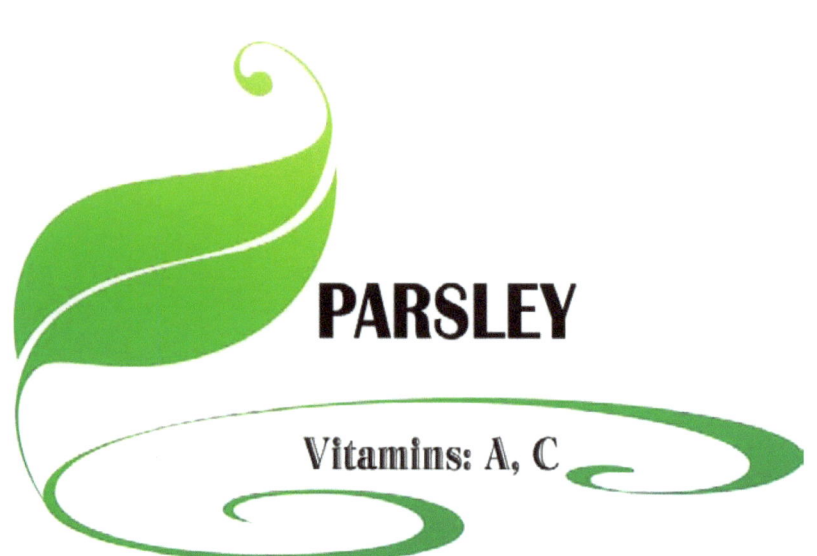

PARSLEY

Vitamins: A, C

PEREJIL

VITAMINAS: A, C

ROSEMARY

Vitamins: A, B12, C

ROMERO

VITAMINAS: A, B12, C

www.ingramcontent.com/pod-product-compliance
Lightning Source LLC
Chambersburg PA
CBHW042315150426
43201CB00001B/9